THE BEAUTY OF
VERMONT

THE BEAUTY OF
VERMONT

Photographs by
Vermont Life Contributing Photographers

Text by
Tom Slayton

A VERMONT LIFE BOOK

Cover photograph and frontispiece: The village of Peacham in autumn, by Alan L. Graham.
Back cover photographs: team in Fairfield, by Paul O. Boisvert; sunflowers in Danby, by Jerry LeBlond;
autumn foliage in Peacham, by Marilyn L. Johnson; snowstorm in Underhill Center, by William H. Johnson.

Printed in the United States of America. First printing, September, 1998. Second printing, June, 1999.

Book design by Eugenie S. Delaney.
Photographs by *Vermont Life* contributing photographers.

Library of Congress Cataloging-in-Publication Data:
The beauty of Vermont / photographs by Vermont Life; contributing photographers;
commentary by Tom Slayton.
p. cm.
ISBN 0-936896-59-0
1. Vermont—Pictorial works. 2. Vermont—Description and travel.
3. Landscape—Vermont—Pictorial works. 4. Landscape photography—Vermont.
I. Slayton, Tom, 1941- . II. Vermont life.
F50.B44 1998
917.4304'43—dc21   98-8208
                                                                    CIP

CONTENTS

INTRODUCTION

A *POPULAR T-SHIRT* proclaims that Vermont is "A State of Nature," and to many visitors that seems to be the whole truth — all those green mountains and green meadows make our state seem a place where nature's beauty has survived in its purest possible form.

But appearances aside, that's not really true.

Vermont was very nearly in a "state of nature," when the Rev. Nathan Perkins of Hartford, Connecticut, struggled through it in 1789, and he hated it with a passion. "Got lost twice in ye woods already," the city-bred minister noted with grim misery in the diary he made of his Vermont trip. "Heard ye horrible howling of ye wolves."

LEFT. Jeffersonville and the Lamoille River, by Zbig Jedrus.
ABOVE: Gloriosa daisies, East Hardwick, by Alan L. Graham.

TOP: Farm equipment, Newark,
by Bob Marinace.
ABOVE: Tools, Addison County,
by Paul O. Boisvert.

Vermont, wild and dangerous in its early years, was gradually domesticated. Nature — much of nature anyway — was tamed and, through prodigious effort transformed into rolling farmland, complete with barns, pastures, farmhouses, roads and villages: rural Vermont. Today, it is that image that strikes a responsive chord in the traveler's breast and pleases Vermonters with the wisdom of their choice of domicile.

Vermont happens to look beautiful today because it is a place where humanity and nature have worked together for more than two centuries. No longer a wilderness that howls, Vermont has become a beautifully woven fabric of small villages and compact cities surrounded by farms and mountains and forestland. It is a middle ground, somewhere between nature-in-the-raw and the over-civilized life — nature completely obliterated — that is all too common in much of America today.

The state's characteristic interplay of village, field and forest, the beauty of its streams and lakes and mountains, give Vermont its sense of place, and are dear to the hearts of newcomer and native alike. Journalist Neill Pearce has dubbed Vermont "the Beloved State" because of the affection nearly everyone seems to harbor for it. Surely one reason for that widespread affection is the pastoral beauty of the Vermont countryside.

Despite the obvious scarring of parts of Vermont's rural landscape and the fringes of some cities and villages here with suburban housing developments and commercial sprawl, most of our state today stands in striking contrast to much of the rest of America. Vermont is still a place: beautiful, cogent, open and green. Its varied landscapes make logical as well as aesthetic sense. I doubt they could exist anywhere else.

There are examples of such landscapes all over the place. Driving west

from Fairfield on Route 36, as you crest the top of the hill above St. Albans, there's suddenly a sweeping view below you of Lake Champlain, the broad Champlain Valley, the little city of St. Albans and a carpet of farm fields interspersed with woodlots. It's a view that most Franklin County residents know and like and probably take in stride — just a part of their world. But it's truly incredible — a spectacular landscape that stands up well when compared to other spectacular landscapes throughout the world.

Driving down Berlin Street in Montpelier, half a mile from the *Vermont Life* offices, I am regularly treated to a stunning view of my little city, the smallest state capital in America, nestled among the forested foothills of the Worcester Range. On one side of town is the gold-domed State House; on the other is the Italianate tower of City Hall. The two buildings stare noncommittally at each other, emphasizing in architecture that state-local tension that defines much of the public life of Montpelier.

Slanting light and a summer farmscape in Barnet, by Alan Jakubek.

9

There are many, many more such views: the lonely Federal elegance of the Hayden Mansion, complete with its legend of a family curse, that dominates a broad field just south of the little village of Albany; the grandeur of Mount Equinox's huge bulk, looming above Manchester Village; the simple beauty of the village of East Corinth; the Victorian opulence of downtown St. Johnsbury; the City of Burlington seen from Lake Champlain — and the lake itself, as it spreads majestically out before you as you descend Burlington's Main Street hill; the dozens of riverscapes you see driving along old Route 5 in the Connecticut River Valley; the intimate village views of Grafton, Weston, Brownington, North Shrewsbury; the delightful little valley of West Arlington — and on and on.

As much of the rest of the urban and suburban Northeast becomes homogenized by highways, franchise restaurants, hamburger palaces and shopping malls, Vermont will become more and more unusual — and more and more sought after.

This book was published to celebrate Vermont's landscape, and to remind us of its importance. For nearly 50 years, *Vermont Life* has presented the Vermont countryside in all its undeniable beauty, as a part of every issue. So we have a vested interest in that countryside's continued beauty and integrity. My belief is that most Vermonters do, too, for three important reasons: Our landscape is important to our economy, to our identity and to our spirit.

The economic importance of landscape to Vermont is growing every day. In an increasingly competitive market for tourists, landscape is one of the unique things Vermont has to offer. We don't have the Rocky Mountains or the Grand Canyon; there's no single spectacular attraction that makes Vermont

ABOVE: Wallace Illsley takes a break during sugaring on his East Braintree farm, by Sandy Macys. LEFT: Waitsfield Common, by Dennis Curran.

stand out. But we do have a gorgeous countryside, one that people from around the world admire and love.

Cultural tourism and ecotourism are the wave of the traveling future, and Vermont stands poised to prosper because of these new trends. Vermont's green countryside, its mountains, small villages, clean rivers and lakes are not only things of beauty — they are attractions to much of the rest of the Northeast. If we allow them to be destroyed or compromised, they can enhance nothing. But if we care for and preserve them, they can enhance our lives and the lives of those visitors who come to be refreshed by them. And obviously, if visitors continue to travel to Vermont, our economy will prosper.

But the land around us is something more than our meal ticket. For one thing, our "working landscape" is the visual expression of our farming heritage. You can see it in the land, in any of a thousand long, beautiful views. And the life lived in Vermont — informal, outdoorsy, farm and village-oriented, is a direct function of that landscape and its lessons about reality, chance, weather and the seasons.

Even though only a tiny portion of us now live on farms, Vermont's farming heritage has contributed much to our sense of who and what we are. The intimate, knowing relationship with land and weather required by farming — to say nothing of the long winters — has clearly shaped the Vermont character. The work ethic that distinguishes Vermont workers was honed on the farm, as were the independence and self-reliance so valued by Vermonters. These little-recognized "products" of our farm heritage offer us more than dollars. They help define our identity.

University of Vermont Professor Frank Bryan once said words to the effect that Vermont without farms would still be a nice place, but it wouldn't

The daily winter windshield scrape,
Lincoln, by Paul O. Boisvert.

be Vermont. And he was right. Not all Vermonters have lived on farms, and a minority of Vermonters now make their living by farming, but we all have learned from our farming neighbors and have been shaped by our closeness to a living agricultural tradition.

Landscape gives us a daily reminder of our rural farming heritage. And it mirrors the fact that Vermont is a real place with real traditions, linked to a real past. In a very immediate sense, it is the emblem of our experience.

If that landscape were lost or badly eroded, as some fear it could be, Vermont would lose not only its prime economic resource in the battle for tourists — it would lose a part of its identity, and perhaps a portion of its soul.

Perhaps the hardest thing to say in this deeply materialistic time is that Vermont's landscape also offers spiritual benefits. Virtually every Vermonter, myself included, has noted that when times get tough, when cabin fever or despair strikes, a walk in the woods or along a country lane helps put things in perspective and offers spiritual refreshment.

Robert Frost, George Aiken, Deane Davis, Dorothy Canfield Fisher and many, many others made the same discovery. A natural landscape is restorative and allows the human spirit to re-create itself. It's a Romantic notion, true, but one founded in the common experience of Vermonters.

TOP: The Tinker farm in Fletcher anchors a drifted winter landscape with Mount Mansfield poking into the clouds in the distance.
ABOVE: Peacham sledders Brendan Gordon and his brother Declan in front of the Town Hall, both by Alan Jakubek.

There are many things that can be done to help preserve the beauty of the Vermont countryside. Vermont's strong body of environmental law has helped. So has the innovative work of land trusts and the advocacy offered by environmental organizations. We should all be grateful for the hard work done every day, over years and lifetimes by Vermont's farmers. They are truly the front-line troops keeping Vermont's working landscape working, and they deserve all our thanks. It makes a difference to those farmers, and to the Vermont countryside if we regularly purchase locally grown food and fiber.

But I'd like to go a step beyond simple preservation and suggest that we think anew about our relationship with land. Rather than simply "saving" the landscape, we need to redefine ourselves in relation to it.

We know that a human relationship is unhealthy when it's based upon exploitation or taking and, conversely, is usually healthy when based upon nurturing and cooperation. In the same way, we can build relationships with the earth that are constructive or destructive. It's easy to tell the difference between a farming relationship to the land, which of necessity involves time and commitment, and a clear-cut-the-timber, subdivide-and-sell relationship.

It's the former, more responsible sort of relationship that Vermonters have traditionally had with their land, and that we need to maintain today. Humanity can live with nature, work with nature, and profit by the association. Vermont's long history proves that. Yet it also proves that we can damage nature — and ourselves — through carelessness, ignorance and greed.

Only if we build careful, nurturing relationships to the land will the land take care of us in turn. Only by loving and caring for our incomparable countryside can we hope to continue to reap the enormous benefits — of economy, heritage and spirit — that it now gives us. ❦

ABOVE: The Windsor-Cornish covered bridge spans the Connecticut, by Jon Gilbert Fox. LEFT: Splendors of the summer at the Old Stone House in Brownington, by William H. Johnson.

Spring in Vermont is the hardest-born season, the one we wait for the longest. Just last March, a sunny day with temperatures close to 50° followed a freezing cold night and was followed, in turn, by a mini-blizzard that left roads a mess and my garage door frozen, again, to its icy sill.

It's that sort of weatherly waywardness that has kept the Puritan ethic burning brightly in our souls. You remember the Puritan ethic? The notion inherited from our forefathers that pleasure is bad, pain is good and, if possible, we should feel guilty about both? Guilt, as my Northeast Kingdom-born wife likes to say, makes good citizens. And so does the hardship of waiting for violets and lilacs and warm days through weeks of overcast skies and grungy, crackling ice. We plow through the days of late winter on autopilot, waiting and waiting.

But there are surprises, even in March. Out walking in the wooded hills above my house not long ago, the temperature was near zero, the wind bitter. Looking for shelter, I slipped into a stand of hemlocks and felt the reassuring chaos of second-growth forest close around me. Tracks crisscrossed in the snow and some papery beech leaves rattled in the breeze. Off on the far side of a clearing a deer bounded away through the thickets.

Some unknown bird called mysteriously and a little later a handful of crows blew over. The forest was quiet but far from lifeless.

After an hour, getting tired, I turned back toward home. Half a mile I trudged, mostly downhill, wrapped in winter. A cold dusk was falling; it would be below zero by the time darkness completely filled my little valley.

LEFT: *Mud season in Adamant,*
by Paul O. Boisvert.
ABOVE: *Cornwall,*
by Clyde H. Smith.

Then, descending through the last snowy twilight, I saw the first sign of spring: The bare branches of willows, scattered along the creek bed below me had, following their ancient timetable, begun to turn bright yellow. A half-dozen webs of golden branches shone in the gathering dusk. Spring might come after all, I told myself.

Town Meeting Day and maple sugaring are the traditional first signs of spring in Vermont. But this year, it snowed, cold and fine, on Town Meeting Day and, after voting, I shoveled snow. I would have to go some other day to look for swelling buds and open streams; some other week I would go count the wisps of steam dotting brown hillsides above each sugarhouse. It would be several weeks before I would happily note the rising tide of green along the brown flanks of the mountains as trees budded and leafed out tenuously, for the first time, and the new foliage climbed higher and higher. No, Town Meeting Day this year was one of the inevitable steps back toward winter, and I contented myself by bringing in more wood for the evening fire.

Yet I knew, as sure as the lengthening days, that soon I would be smelling raw earth and fresh manure on the wind. Soon the rush of open streams, the yelling of kids at play outdoors, even the first birds — probably the harsh, welcome screaming of red-winged blackbirds down in the swamp — would greet my ears. Already the crows are sculling about the neighborhood again, picking over the frozen compost pile, creating mischief. And that earliest spring smell, the cold, moist smell of thawing snow, is about on warmer days.

Maple buds have already swelled and the osiers have turned bright red again. They remind me of Henry David Thoreau, because he called them

ABOVE: Record of a season at Robert Howrigan's sugarhouse, Fairfield.
RIGHT: Members of the Howrigan family make the rounds to hang buckets, Fairfield, both by Paul O. Boisvert.

"winter fruit," and wrote about them affectionately. In his voluminous journals, Thoreau recorded the appearance of skunk cabbage and the catkins of swamp maples. He even described precisely the atmosphere of these earliest spring days.

"The hardness of winter is relaxed," he wrote on March 10, 1859. "There is a fine effluence surrounding the wood, as if the sap had begun to stir and you could detect it a mile off. Such is the difference between an object seen through a warm, moist, soft air and a cold, dry, hard one. Such is the genialness of nature that the trees appear to have put out feelers by which the senses apprehend them more tenderly."

ABOVE: *Geese on parade in Woodstock, by Kindra Clineff.*
LEFT: *Shadows stretch across fields in Windsor, by Alan L. Graham.*

Thoreau concluded: "I do not know that the woods are ever more beautiful, or affect me more."

For generations, New Englanders have savored these early notices of spring, held them to heart and taken hope from them. We need them, to survive the rag-end of winter and start the cycle of life once again.

Fortunately, they are there every year, just for the taking. 🌿

ABOVE: A fly fisherman along
the Mettawee River
in southwestern Vermont,
by Alden Pellett.
LEFT: Ewell Pond in Peacham,
by George Cahoon Jr.

ABOVE: *Tulip garden in Woodstock,*
by Alan L. Graham.
LEFT: *Leaves uncurl on a Pomfret*
farm, by Allen Karsh.

ABOVE: *Starksboro,
by Paul O. Boisvert.*
RIGHT: *Spring at
Perfect Maple Farm in
East Montpelier, by André Jenny.*

ABOVE· Magnolia in Manchester,
by Alden Pellett.
LEFT. Hepatica, by Ted Levin.
FAR LEFT: Spring comes to Danby,
by Alan L. Graham.

ABOVE: Columbine, by Ted Levin.
LEFT: Burnham Hollow Orchard
in the hills of Middletown Springs,
by Jerry LeBlond.

SUMMER

SUMMER IS VERMONT'S shortest season. It lasts a scant dozen or so weeks, from the chilly nights of early June to the chilly nights of late August, but while it is here, Vermonters rightly prize each day. Summer days are a rare commodity, and everyone wishes there were just a few more or that they could somehow last just a little longer.

In this brief season, the outdoors is more welcoming than at any other time of the year. And Vermonters respond in kind; we live outdoors so much that we almost become a part of the landscape: moving, breathing components of the larger assembly, fishing the brooks, swimming in the lakes and rivers, gardening and haying, cooking in the back yard, climbing

---

LEFT: Sunflowers in Danby, by Jerry LeBlond.
ABOVE: Window box, Charlotte, by Patricia Miller.

TOP: Route 140 in Tinmouth, by Jerry LeBlond.
ABOVE & RIGHT: Forest overtakes the abandoned hill farms of Little River State Park's Ricker Basin, by Alan L. Graham.

the mountains, sleeping under the stars.

Winter has stark beauty; spring, exuberance and romance; autumn, its sweet melancholy; but summer is more straightforward. It simply opens the door, draws us into the greater world of nature, and seems glad to have us there.

The hours of high summer are numbered. The obvious approach is to seize them and fill them with activity while they last — cram as much as you can into every sunlit hour. Get your work done early so you can get in a bike trip to the lake, a picnic while there, and a swim before pedaling speedily home. That may be what gives summer its frantic edge: We know that all too soon the long July days will yield to the cool evenings of September.

Unfortunately, that only seems to make the days go by faster.

There is a more measured approach. It's called contemplation, an art mastered by an older generation of Vermonters. They have long known that filling the hours with activity only makes them speed by. To slow the days down, you've got to slow yourself down.

Years ago when she was a girl, my mother and her family had a way of decelerating time. At dusk, they would just stop, and sit. Usually this happened on the porch of the little farmhouse where they lived. First the children, then the older ones would come to the porch after supper, as the day began to wane. They would just sit there without saying much of anything and watch it get dark, savoring the summer twilight like a glass of fine wine. (It was, needless to say, the only wine they savored.)

Loosestrife and poppies bloom in South Reading, by Tom Narwid.

I used to watch my grandmother on summer afternoons as she tended her rock garden. She was a busy woman, with all the responsibilities that being a partner in a small farming operation would suggest. Yet she still found time to garden, and while there, she never hurried. There was a lot of time between each task given to the simple appreciation of each flower, each moment of the long afternoon. She knew how to make time move with delicious slowness.

The key to making summer last is to do not more, but less; we need to take the time to appreciate the bright, dappled sky, the mottled sunlight on the hills. And to listen: for the laughter of kids playing, the ever-present sounds of work: hammers and saws and tractors and passing cars. Though the birds have subsided since their spring breeding madness, the conversation of weather with the land is constant: the rush of wind that rustles tree leaves and predicts the coming of a rainstorm, the drowsy hum of a meadow baking in the July heat, the cool green whispering of a forest at midday.

Finally, dusk gathers us in and unites us with the greater world. Usually we head for home, companionship, a lighted space and the security of shelter — or at least a campfire and a tent. But wisdom counsels us not to resist evening completely.

After some sunsets, we need to be gathered with the land into the warm living darkness of a summer night. We rarely choose those times; rather, they choose us. Twilight fades from the gently moving surface of the lake, glimmers and is gone. The wind rustles softly through the surrounding trees, as if arranging its possessions one last time before sleep. The details of the forest and then the shore gradually disappear.

The stars come out. We feel the edges of our being blur, ever so slightly, and we know we are a part of the wide universe. The world has, for the moment, accepted us. It would be unseemly to scorn its hospitality.

Contented, we splash our toes gently in the warm, dark waters. 🏵

Lilac blossoms offer their spring beauty in Randolph Center, top, and at Shelburne Museum, above, both by Alan L. Graham.

41

ABOVE: The West Arlington
covered bridge over the Batten Kill,
Vermont Department
of Tourism & Marketing.
LEFT: Jeffersonville, by Tom Narwid.

ABOVE: *Summer play*
in Ripton, by Alan Jakubek.
RIGHT: *Guilford,*
by William H. Johnson.

ABOVE: Kettle Pond, Groton
State Forest, by André Jenny.
RIGHT & FAR RIGHT: Shelburne
Bay, by Paul O. Boisvert.

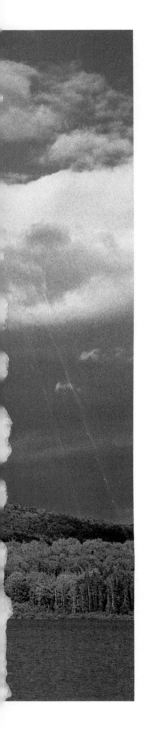

ABOVE: A fly fisherman casts
into the Lamoille River near
Fairfax, by Alan Jakubek.
LEFT: Bull moose,
by Charles H. Willey.
FAR LEFT: Canoeist on
Marshfield Pond below Marshfield
Ledges, by Alden Pellett.

ABOVE: Asiatic lilies at Floral
Gates Nursery, Guilford,
by Alan L. Graham.
LEFT: Shaftsbury farm,
by Jon-Pierre Lasseigne.

*ABOVE: Ringside seat,
Addison County Field Days,
New Haven, by Alden Pellett.
LEFT: Strawberry harvest,
Newfane, by Paul Miller.
FAR LEFT: Late Summer mist
in Danby Four Corners,
by Alan L. Graham.*

TOP: Jocelyn Peknik,
volunteer farmhand on the
Major Farm in Westminster West,
by S. Michael Bisceglie.
ABOVE: Farmers' market harvest,
by Jon Gilbert Fox.
RIGHT: Whiting, by Lynn M. Stone.

A U T U M N

D ESPITE THE BEAUTY of a Vermont autumn, despite the spectacular shades of red and orange, despite the invigorating chill in the mornings and evenings and the gentle mists that seep from the hillsides into the valleys — despite all that and more — my hunch is that most Vermonters are not passionately in love with fall.

We enjoy the beauty of the season, to be sure. But those of us who live here know that for all its beauty, autumn is a time of growing darkness that presages winter. To me, the season feels a bit melancholy. Perhaps it's all those years of giving up summer for the return to school. Perhaps

LEFT: Lefferts Pond and Blue Ridge Mountain,
Chittenden, by William H. Johnson.
ABOVE: The colors of maple, Norwich, by Jon Gilbert Fox.

ABOVE: Pumpkins for sale, Monkton, by Paul O. Boisvert. RIGHT: Autumn descends on Ryegate, by Marilyn S. Rogers.

it's thoughts of heavy coats and snow tires and all the logistics of winter again. Perhaps it's just the knowledge that my two big maple trees are going to dump upwards of 1,000 pounds of leaves on my lawn and that, beautiful though they are, they will all have to be piled and bagged.

Noel Perrin tells the story of one of his neighbors, a farmer, who was approached by a beaming television crew from Boston who asked him, on camera, if he didn't just love the beautiful color of the leaves this time of year.

"Makes me think of winter," said the farmer. "My favorite time of year is blossom time."

So much for leafy sentimentality. Part of my problem with the foliage season is that it is so quickly over. Vermont's most spectacular display of natural beauty is also its most transient. In less than a month, the brilliant colors of fall produce the whirlwind of activity that is Vermont's most intense tourist season.

Expectation builds and builds as September moves into October. Will it be a good foliage year? When will peak color come? Where should we go? What should we see? And then within two or, at the most, three weeks, it's over, color having ignited and burned through our region like a brief, bright torch.

We drive over Pudding Hill in Lyndonville or skirt the sides of the Mad River Valley, or make our way down to West Arlington, and marvel at the eloquent beauty of October. Then the leaves begin to fall, and days already shortened begin to drop whole chunks of daylight minutes off into the gathering darkness. Hiking in the mountains, though unbelievably beautiful, becomes a bit more schedule-bound. You don't really want to spend a night in the woods in October.

The brightest colors last only a few weeks; by November, they are pretty much a memory. However, those who have watched several autumns

come and go know that there is not one foliage season, but three, perhaps four, each with its own beauty. They follow one another from late September until mid-November.

First there is the early show of a few bright, preliminary trees, displaying their colors against the brassy-green, late summer hillsides. More and more trees change color until the precise moment (usually in early October) when it seems the color has reached its richest.

The exact day — or moment — when Vermont's annual display of fall color will be at its most brilliant is one of Vermont's perennial mysteries. Just when will the foliage peak? There are foliage reports on every radio station and in all the newspapers, and plenty of speculation about "peak foliage." But no one ever seems to know for sure when the peak is until after it happens. That's because while it is the height of fall color, peak color is also a shifting, half-illusory phenomenon, perhaps even a mystical state, not simply an act of nature.

Every year the timing is slightly different; every year the colors vary in intensity. Generally, it begins in northern Vermont and at higher altitudes, where the nights turn frosty earlier in the year. It sweeps southward through the state in late September and early October. At last the precise moment arrives when it seems the leaves just can't get any brighter. Camera shutters snap all over Vermont. Whole mountainsides of color call to the hiker, and the woods themselves have an acrid, tangy smell, the smell that frost brings to fallen leaves.

Not long afterward a steady autumn rain or a day of high wind, or both, are sure to fade the vivid reds and oranges to pastel. These softer, subtler colors sometimes last into November, turning to pale yellows and somber browns before the leaves finally fall, leaving the hillsides to November's muted grays and purples.

The subtler glories of fall's last colors are not appreciated by everyone. Yet, for many, the prettiest time of the year is late autumn — the final foliage season — when the leaves fade and fall and the hillsides take on quiet, velvety hues.

It's a lovely season, one that many longtime Vermonters know intimately and enjoy. Perhaps our affection for November stems from the fact that the tourists attracted by October's reds and oranges have gone away and the hills are left for those committed to life here year-round to appreciate. Or perhaps we simply like the stark, elemental beauty that settles in along with the late-season chill and the smell of wood smoke.

ABOVE: The colors of the season fall on carefully placed stones in Townshend, by Paul R. Turnbull. LEFT: Waitsfield cow-crossing, by Dennis Curran.

Morning fog lifts in Lower Waterford, by Alan L. Graham.

It's the subtler colors that dominate November. The mountains sit in meditative rows, subdued forms of blue and gray along the edges of each valley. The yellow corn has been harvested, chopped, and siloed. Only rows of stubble remain. The night comes early and stays long. All life is subdued now; the seasons of growth are over for another year.

The entire countryside has begun preparing for a long winter's nap and, to the watchful eye, the signs of the season are everywhere.

For humankind, fall is a time of chores. There are leaves to be raked, stovepipes to be checked, windows and doors to be tightened. The days are shorter, and mornings have that crisp chill that tells you it's time to make sure your wood supply is close at hand and dry. (It's much too late now to start cutting wood, but you can restack it, if you like.)

On the farm, the never-ending flow of work becomes even more urgent, as cows are put in barns and everyone prepares for several months of tending to "the girls" indoors. The last of the harvest is collected and stored. Animals are butchered. Food is dried or canned or blanched and frozen.

The preparations that nature makes as fall deepens and winter edges closer are overwhelming. Every fallen leaf is a tiny chlorophyll factory, shut down after a long season of hard work. Grasses and ferns wither and turn golden; a hint of wood smoke — or is it mist? — hangs in the afternoon air, and soon flocks of Canada and snow geese can be seen wending their primordial way southward. Many other birds migrate, of course — even monarch butterflies gather and flutter toward Mexico, taking sustenance from the last flowers of the year as they go.

The season closes down gradually, a day at a time. Autumn finally closes, not with a feeling of loss or abandonment, but rather of completion. A huge task has been gracefully done, every bit of it. Time now to build the season's first fire in the woodstove.

Autumn colors frame a window in North Calais, by Alan L. Graham.

Everything seems to hold its breath, waiting for snow, for winter, for the long white sleep so necessary for rebirth.

*ABOVE: On the road to Lake
Champlain, West Milton,
by Paul O. Boisvert.
RIGHT: East Montpelier,
by C.B. Johnson.*

ABOVE: In the hills near Ludlow,
by Jerry LeBlond.
LEFT: Peacham,
by Marilyn L. Johnson.

ABOVE: *The Strafford Town House,*
by Kindra Clineff.
RIGHT: *Echo Lake in Tyson,*
by Jerry LeBlond.

ABOVE: *The Jenne Farm,*
Reading, by Mary Clay.
LEFT: *Peacham, by Alden Pellett.*

71

TOP LEFT: Monarch butterfly,
by Andrea A. Wilson.
TOP RIGHT: Blue jay, Calais,
by Tim Seaver.
ABOVE: Frosted leaves,
by Lois Moulton.
FAR RIGHT: Sugar maples in
Reading, by William H. Johnson.

ABOVE: East Topsham,
by Alan L. Graham.
LEFT: A working landscape, Cabot,
by Alan L. Graham.

WINTER

*T*HESE ARE THE DARK DAYS, the January
days, the days of ice and thaw and misery, when we rise in the dark
and come home in the dark, and winter's grip seems interminable. I
sometimes wonder in January what summer could possibly have been like.

I've never liked the depths of midwinter much; and, in fact, neither
has humanity in general. It's just a function of that little polar tilt of our
earth's axis, and the resulting seasonal differences probably make it
possible for life to survive here at all. Yet something deep in our alligator
brains sees the sun disappearing, sees plants die, sees the ice and snow

---

LEFT: A cold morning dawns in Worcester, by Alden Pellett.
ABOVE: Skating on Lake Champlain,
South Hero, by Paul O. Boisvert.

deepening, the chill descending, and looks for ways to escape.

All the darkness and cold force us inside, where we can think too many long, dark thoughts. Christmas was obviously invented by the Pagans and adopted by the Christians to take our minds off these bare days that begin, grudgingly, at 7 and end, without apology, at 4:30.

Granted, when the sun does shine and there's snow, there's nothing more gorgeous than Vermont's rolling pastoral countryside, glistening in the bright, crisp cold. But last winter there just wasn't that much full sun, and instead of snow, December gave us rain that in January froze into gray concrete. This cancelled the cross-country skiing and left me itching for activity.

And so, not far into January, I turned on all the Christmas lights — still up, in futile protest against the gloom — and went for a walk in the gathering afternoon twilight. My destination was Montpelier's Hubbard Park. I knew I would find nature there; sleeping to be sure, but nature still.

ABOVE: *East Topsham woodpile, by Alan L. Graham.*
RIGHT: *Hartford, by Paul Rezendes.*

And so I did. I walked up the hill to the park, which was once a hilltop pasture but has now reverted to woods. I left the pavement behind, and the crunch of icy snow underfoot guided me along the park's narrow trails. I wasn't alone: A jogger toiled past me, her cheeks glowing in the chill. I trudged along and passed a parked car with the motor running and someone sitting patiently within its heated interior.

I turned onto a seldom-used path to get away from the park road, and the hard snow crunched beneath my boots. The cold made my ears and nose tingle. The dark shapes of trees and rocky ledges covered with snow

surrounded me and I left them, one by one, behind. The darkness began to deepen and I felt a quiet calm gather within me. The woods had begun, once again, their process of soothing and healing

I emerged from the trees and walked along a flat stretch of park road that overlooks Montpelier's little downtown. Most of the year, that bit of road is a leafy tunnel shielded from the city below by the forest.

But on that wintry day, with the leaves long gone, the bare trees simply framed the streets and houses below, and as I walked along the road, I could see the living city spread out before me, its streetlights coming on as evening came on, cars passing the lighted houses and the twinkling of lights on streets farther and farther away. A door slammed, and I heard voices, far off, indistinct yet somehow crisp in the winter evening air.

We all too often tell ourselves that people and nature are two different things — that people somehow spoil nature or, conversely, that nature must, after all, make way for people. But looking down on the city twinkling below me as the stars began to twinkle above, I had a different thought.

We are not two different things, I thought: we're the same thing. There is a place for us in nature — if we know our place. Just as there has to be a place for nature in the human scheme of things. It's all in the balance and in having the humility to know our own limits.

When we can know both the husbanded beauty of our own little village, winking awake in the wintry dusk, and the larger, wilder beauty of the dark trees, the falling snow, and the darkening sky above — when we can know and accept both — then we may find a way to live in this world without ruining it.

It was a good enough thought for January, so I walked it through the streets and home with me. And now, I offer it to you. 🌿

ABOVE: *Antique gas pumps in the town of Orange.*
LEFT: *New snow on a hillside farm in East Montpelier, both by André Jenny.*

ABOVE: Snow and Christmas in Guilford, by C.B. Johnson.
LEFT: Cardinal in Dorset, by David Kutchukian.
FAR LEFT: Snowstorm in Underhill Center, by William H. Johnson.

ABOVE: *Dog sled racing in Stowe,*
by Alan L. Graham.
RIGHT: *Sleds, by Jon Gilbert Fox.*
FAR RIGHT: *Sliding on Casey's*
Hill, Underhill, by Paul O. Boisvert

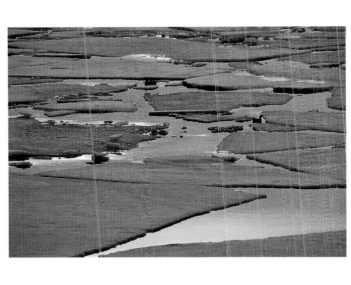

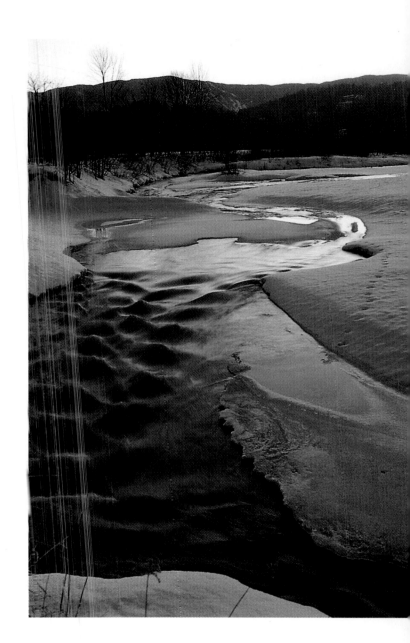

TOP: *Break-up,*
by Michael M. Stetson.
RIGHT: *Winter flow on the*
Mad River, by Jerry LeBlond.
LEFT & ABOVE: *Sunset on Lake*
Champlain in Charlotte,
and hard-water sailing,
both by Paul O. Boisvert.

*ABOVE: Putney horseman
Maynard Aiken with
Toby and Dick,
by S. Michael Bisceglie.
LEFT: The full glory of a sunny
winter day in Warren,
by Alan L. Graham.*

ABOVE: *Ice fishing on Echo Lake in Tyson, by George F. Neary.*
RIGHT: *Aaron Machia and northern pike, Lake Champlain, by Paul O. Boisvert.*
FAR RIGHT: *Ken Gokey shovels off a roof in Cabot, by Alan L. Graham.*

92